# A LITTLE RELAXATION...

by Dr. Saul Miller

HARTLEY & MARKS PUBLISHERS

Published
in the U.S.A. by
Hartley & Marks Inc.
P.O. Box 147
Point Roberts, WA
98282

Published
in Canada by
Hartley & Marks Ltd.
3663 West Broadway
Vancouver, B.C.
V6R 2B8

Typeset by The Typeworks
Printed in the USA
Cover art by Janis Merendino

I wish to acknowledge some synergy
in the creative process and thank the following:
Dr. JoAnne Miller my wife and colleague who inspired,
guided, and prodded me towards A Little Relaxation. Leonard Orr,
Marjorie Barstow, Walter Carrington, Edmund Jacobson, who shared
their ideas and techniques. David Sievers, Kolin Lymworth,
Charlene Koonce, and Mary Speck for suggestions and
support. Victor Marks, Sue Tauber, and Susan Kerr,
a creative band at Hartley & Marks who helped
me put some thoughts and a rhythm
between two covers.

LIBRARY OF CONGRESS
CATALOGING-IN PUBLICATION DATA

Miller, Saul. (Saul B.)
A little relaxation  /  by Saul Miller.
ISBN 0-88179-025-7  :  $7.95
1.  Relaxation.   I.  Title.
RA785.M54   1990
613.7'9--dc20

To Morris and Anne

The word "relax" comes from the Latin word *laxus* which means to be loose.
To relax simply means to regain a natural feeling of looseness and ease.

Relaxation is a mind—body process with many benefits.
It lowers heart rate and blood pressure.
It improves respiratory efficiency.
It reduces muscle tension.
It allows more energy to flow.
It increases stress tolerance.

Relaxing is balancing.
It feels good.
It helps us to recharge.
It promotes health, healing, and longevity.

Relaxing also enhances the function of our brain and
nervous system.
It balances the activity of the left and right cerebral
hemispheres.
It improves the quality of our thoughts and images.
It reduces "mental static".
It enhances perception, awareness, memory and judgment.
It brings more ease and pleasure to the moment.

The bottom line
Relaxation supports your total well-being and the way you
perform.

There are many approaches to relaxation. The dynamic relaxation technique that follows is something I've developed and used with some of the world's top performers in sports, business, and the arts.

*Dynamic relaxation is for everyone.*

Dynamic relaxation is a way to release and recharge.
The technique will enable you to release "blocks"
and draw more power to you.
It will connect you with the energy field around you.
And, it will support you in expressing yourself with greater effectiveness, ease, and pleasure in whatever you do.

Dynamic relaxation is a way to stay calm and focused.
You can use this little relaxation book to learn how
to take a five minute "power break," or you can use the principle of release... breathe... and refocus
in managing yourself with more grace and efficiency throughout the day.

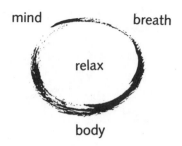

mind     breath

relax

body

There are three elements to the dynamic relaxation process.
First. . . relaxed breathing
Second. . . relaxed body
Third. . . relaxed mind

In the book I describe each of these elements separately.
In reality, they all blend and work together.
Breath is a link between mind and body.

As you tune into your breathing, allow your awareness to
expand to include the rise and fall of your physical body
and the flow of energy to you and through you.
As you breathe, feel yourself releasing tension
and becoming calmer and clearer.

Relaxing the body calms the mind.
Calming the mind harmonizes bodily function, feels
comfortable, and enables us to breathe more freely
and easily.

*Dynamic relaxation combines free breathing
with "good feeling" and empowering thoughts.*

clear
thinking

free
breathing

relaxed

good
feeling

To begin, make yourself comfortable.
Sit or lie back.
Uncross your arms and your legs.
Allow the weight of your body to be supported
by whatever you're resting on.
Tune into your breathing.

## BREATHE EASY

Breathing is one of the easiest, and most effective ways
to regulate the emotions.
Using your breathing you can energize or tranquilize
yourself. You can use breathing to clear and focus the
mind.

If you're upset, "speeding," angry, sad, or depressed,
focus on your breathing.
An effective relaxing technique is to breathe "connecting"
the inbreath to the outbreath. . . the outbreath to the
inbreath. . . the inbreath to the outbreath. . . the outbreath
to the inbreath. . .

You can do it sitting or lying down, walking, or moving
around.

# RELAX THE BREATH

Relax and breathe.
Your breath is like waves in the ocean.
Just as the ocean waves come in... and go out...
with a certain rhythm,
your breath has a wavelike rhythm of its own.
Tune into the natural rhythm of your breath.
Give yourself time for the inbreath to come all the way in.
Give yourself time for the outbreath to go all the way out.

The waves never rush.
Don't rush the breath.
You deserve your time.

*Don't rush the breath.*
*The waves never rush.*

Relax and tune into the rhythm of your breath.
Follow the inbreath (the inwave) all the way in . . .
until it becomes an outbreath (an outwave).
Follow the outbreath all the way out . . .
until it becomes an inbreath.

The waves never rush.
Don't rush the breath.

Let the inbreath become an outbreath.
Let the outbreath become an inbreath.

There's power in rhythm.
There's power in taking your time.

You deserve your time.

*You deserve your time.*
*You deserve your time.*
*You deserve your time.*


Throughout *A Little Relaxation* I repeat the idea
"you deserve...."
The deserve I'm referring to is not something you have to
earn... or a punishment.
It's your birthright.
It's there for you just because you are alive.
You are a **human being**... not a human doing.
You don't have to do something to be.
Simply being you... is enough.

To deserve is a state of feeling worthy.
There is no thing you are more worthy or deserving of
than your time.
Taking time to breathe is an expression of self-love.
It's a key to well-being.
You deserve to feel good.
You deserve love.
These things are natural.


Experience more ease, love, and power in your life.
Give yourself time for the breath to come in...
and go out.


You deserve your time.


12

*Create a relaxed feeling and*
*support it with an empowering thought.*

Dynamic relaxation is about creating a relaxed feeling
and then relating that feeling to an empowering thought.
It's about giving yourself time for the breath to come all the
way in . . . and giving yourself time for the breath to go all
the way out.
It's about acknowledging that when it comes to your
thoughts and feelings you're the boss . . .
and the boss deserves his or her time.

You deserve your time.

Relax and breathe.
Now, guide your attention to the inbreath.
Feel yourself drawing in energy.

Each of us has a personal connection to an
unlimited supply of energy.
With each breath relax and breathe in some of that
energy.
Focus on drawing in power.
The outbreath will look after itself.

*Relax and breathe in energy.*

Inspiration means to draw in spirit or life energy.
Inspire yourself.
With each breath feel yourself drawing in energy.
With each breath you can affirm your aliveness and
direction.

You deserve to feel good.

*Inspire yourself.*
*You deserve to feel good.*

Whatever you're doing...
wherever you are...
whoever you're with...
inspire yourself.
Draw in energy.
You deserve to feel good.
You deserve to express your ability.

*You can erase tension, tiredness, disease,*
*and negativity... with your breath.*

Relax and breathe.
As you do, experience the continuous wave after wave
quality of your breath.

The ocean waves are continuous.
Over time they can wash anything away.
You can wash away tension, tiredness, and negativity
just by tuning into your breathing.

Experience the wave after wave quality of your breathing.
Experience the inwave become an outwave.
Experience the outwave become an inwave.
The waves never stop.

*Connect the inbreath to the outbreath*
*the outbreath to the inbreath.*

Another way to appreciate the continuity of the breath
is to experience your breath as a wheel.
On the inbreath the wheel turns up...
on the outbreath the wheel turns down.

Connect the inbreath to the outbreath...
the outbreath to the inbreath.
Experience your breath as an endlessly turning wheel.
Like the waves, the wheel never stops.

*Experience the breath as a wheel.*
*On the inbreath the wheel turns up...*
*on the outbreath the wheel turns down...*

Whenever you experience a challenging moment,
whenever you have doubt or negativity,
whenever you experience tension and fatigue...
focus your breathing on drawing in energy
and turning the wheel.

A key to dynamic relaxation and to transforming stress into
power is **using** the situation to release and breathe...
to turn the wheel and generate more energy.

Go back to your breathing.
Draw in energy.
Turn the wheel.
Generate power.

Relax and breathe.
The nature of the mind is to focus on something specific.
Focus your attention on the point where the breath
changes direction.
As other thoughts come to mind. . . notice them,
and let them go.
Then guide your attention back to the breath.

For thousands of years people have been looking for ways
to relax, and to calm and clear the mind. One of the most
effective ways is simply to focus attention on a single
stimulus. . . a word, a phrase, a candle, a picture.
There's no stimulus that is more powerful, more personal,
more of the moment, or more integrating than the breath.

Relax and breathe.
Follow your breath in to the peak... and release.
The point where the breath changes direction is a power point.
Make it a focal point.
As other thoughts come to mind... let them go.
Bring your attention back to your breathing.
Follow the inbreath all the way in... to the peak...
and release.
Follow the outbreath all the way out.

You can wash away tension, tiredness, dis-ease, and negativity
wave after wave...
breath after breath.

*Relax and breathe.*
*There is only this breath.*


Relax and breathe.
Tune into the point where the breath changes direction.
Tune into the crest of the wave.
Experiencing your breath like this again and again . . .
connects mind and body.
It integrates your left and right "brains" (cerebral
hemispheres).
It brings you back into the moment.
It enables you to feel and perform at your best.


What's important to remember, is that anxiety and worry
live in the past. . .
"I should (or shouldn't) have done that,"
and in the future. . .
"what'll happen if. . .?"
However, **the power is in the present.**
One way to stay in the moment and where the action is,
is to focus on this breath.

*Experience this breath.*
*The power is in the moment.*

Relax and breathe.
Tune into the point where the breath changes direction.
Follow your breath in to the peak... and release.
As you do, you'll be experiencing this breath.

Experience this breath.
The power is in the moment.
The power is with you.

## USING BREATHING

If you find yourself lying in bed awake . . . worrying about
an important upcoming event (a meeting, a competition, an
exam, a presentation), a relationship, or something you did
or didn't do, simply relax and breathe.
Turn the wheel. Use the situation as a reminder to go back
to the natural rhythm of your breath.


If you're worried about things of the dead past or the
imagined future, release and **breathe**.
Be aware that it's you who are upsetting yourself.
Then, shift your focus to your breathing.
Pick up your breathing rhythm.
Give yourself time for the inbreath to come all the way in.
Give yourself time for the outbreath to go all the way out.
The waves never rush.
You deserve your time.


Experience your personal connection to unlimited energy.
Feel yourself breathing in energy . . . drawing in power.
You deserve to feel good.

Remember, worry is not of the present.
It's of the past . . . and the future.
Stay in the moment. Stay with the breath.
If your mind drifts, guide your attention back to the point
where the breath changes direction.


Stay with the continuous wave after wave quality of your
breathing.
Turn the wheel.
Allow yourself to relax.
You deserve to feel good.

As we said earlier, breathing is one of the easiest and most effective ways to energize or tranquilize yourself...
and to clear and focus the mind.
If you're upset, speeding, angry, sad, or depressed, release and breathe.
"Connect" the inbreath to the outbreath...
the outbreath to the inbreath.
Draw in energy.
Turn the wheel.

Experience
a little relaxation.
Relax and breathe.
Take six connected breaths.
As you do, tune into your breathing rhythm.
With each breath, feel yourself drawing in energy.
Experience the point where the breath changes direction.
Connect the inbreath to the outbreath . . . the outbreath to
the inbreath.
Allow the waves to wash away tension, anger, dis-ease,
and negativity.
Allow yourself to relax and recharge.


Five or six times a day, and whenever you want to relax . . .
tune into your breathing.
Take six "connected" breaths.
Remember, you deserve to feel good.
It's your choice.

*release* = *real ease*

# RELAX THE BODY

Relaxing isn't about trying to do something,
it's about allowing something to happen.
The second phase of dynamic relaxation focuses on
releasing unnecessary tension and **allowing** the body to
relax. In order to enhance your awareness and your ability
to release tension, I'm going to show you a simple tension-
release process (with six different muscle groups).

Many relaxation and stress management techniques use a
tension-release process to help people to relax. Something
unique about this approach is that **in dynamic relaxation
we combine the release of tension with breathing...**
and with thinking an empowering and relaxing thought.

Also, keep in mind that the tension-release process is only a
brief, temporary stage of developing your "release reflex."
It's something you repeat five or ten times as part of
learning how to create a little relaxation... anywhere,
and at any time.

Before we focus on release, remember, a key to relaxing is
reminding yourself that you deserve to feel good, that it's
your body, and that you control the switch.

*Relax your hands.*
*Release and breathe.*

Relaxing the body: hands

Relax and breathe.
To begin the tension-release process
guide attention to your hands.
The hands are an area over which we have great awareness
and control. They're an excellent place to begin.

Make fists... not too tight.
It is the subtle levels of tension that it's important
to become aware of, to control, and to minimize.
Feel the tension in the center of your hand
and in your fingers.
Hold it (three to four seconds).
Then, release... and breathe.

It's the feeling of release and breathe that you want to
experience, recall, and recreate.

Once again tense the fists.
This time also turn in the wrists to exaggerate the feeling
of tension.
Hold it (three to four seconds).
Now release and breathe.
Remember, you deserve to feel good.
And, you control the switch.

Some therapists begin by tensing and releasing the feet
and working their way up. I find it easier and more relaxing
to start with the hands and then move down through the
body.

*Relax the neck and shoulders.*
*Release and breathe.*

Relaxing the body: neck and shoulders

Next, guide attention to your neck and shoulders.
The neck and shoulders are a primary tension holding area.
For most people this is **the** principal tension spot in their
bodies.

Raise your shoulders up (two to three inches)
towards your ears.
Feel the tension in your neck and shoulders.
Hold it (three to four seconds).
Now let it go . . . and take a breath.
That's the feeling of release you want to experience.

*Release tension in the neck and shoulders.*
*Release and breathe.*

Once again, raise up your shoulders.
This time raise them up only a quarter inch.
It's a minimal contraction, but you can feel the tension.
Hold it (three to four seconds).
Release and breathe.
You control the switch.

Mind and body are one.
Every time you have a negative thought
("Oh no," "no way ," "what if," "yeah but. . . ")
there's a slight tensing in the body.
Be aware of that tension.
Release it.
Take a breath.
Then, think an empowering thought.
Think, "I'm o.k."
"I'm the boss."
"I deserve to feel good."
"It's my body."
"It's my choice."

*Relax the face and jaw.*
*Release and breathe.*

Relaxing the body: the jaw

The jaw is another primary tension area.
Many people hold tension and anger in their jaws.
Guide attention to your jaw.
Clench your teeth.
Now curl your lips back to expose your teeth.
Feel the tension that creates in your face.
Hold it (three to four seconds).
Release tension... and breathe.
Think, "I control the switch."

Remember, an important quality of dynamic relaxation
is supporting the feeling of release by taking a breath
and thinking a relaxing, empowering thought.
Thoughts like, "Release and breathe," "I deserve my time,"
"I deserve to feel good," "I control the switch," and
"It's my choice," all work very well.

*Relax and breathe.*
*Smile.*

A genuine smile is like a burst of sunshine.
It is a natural, and pleasurable way to release.
A fake smile is not; it's a reflection of tension.

Create a fake smile.
As you do, feel the mask of tension that creates in the face.
People often react to a fake smile with anger and dis-ease.
That's because tension leads to tension . . .
unless, you use it to trigger release.

Whenever you notice others, or experience yourself with a
tense, fake, "social" smile, release . . . and breathe.
Remember, you don't have to impress anyone to feel good
about yourself.
You'll feel better and perform more effectively by being
more at ease.
Relax, take a breath, and smile.

*Relax and breathe.*
*Allow your chest and abdomen to be free*
*to expand and contract.*

Relaxing the body: chest and abdomen

Guide attention to your chest and abdomen.
Allow the muscles there to be free to expand and contract
with each breath you take.

Relax and breathe.
Place a hand on your upper chest, and one on your lower
abdomen.
As you breathe feel the hands on your chest and abdomen
rise and fall with each wave of your breath.
Feel yourself drawing in energy,
wave after wave.
Give yourself time for the inbreath to become an outbreath.
You deserve your time.
You deserve to feel good.

I often use this technique.
Just putting a hand on my chest is a reminder to breathe.

*Breath is power.*
*Release and breathe.*


Tension is dis-ease.


With your hands on your chest and abdomen, raise your
shoulders half an inch.
Feel the tension in your neck and shoulder muscles.
Hold it. . . .
Notice that you've cut down your breathing.
Release. . . and breathe.


Breath is life and power.
Tensing any part of your body cuts down your breathing
and your energy.
Whenever you feel tension. . . release and breathe. . .
turn the wheel.
Use the tension as a stimulus or a reminder that will trigger
your "release reflex". . . and generate energy.
The bottom line
You deserve to feel good.
You'll feel better and perform better as you release
your dis-ease.
And, you control the switch.

*Release tension in the genitals.*
*Release and breathe.*

Relaxing the body: the genitals

The genitals are another primary tension-holding area.

Relax and breathe.
Guide attention to your sexual organs.
There's a sphincter muscle in the genitals
that we squeeze when holding back in sex, in going to the
toilet, and when we feel defensive and uptight.
Gently tighten that sphincter.
Feel the tension.
Hold it (four to five seconds).
Release . . . and breathe.
That's the feeling to remember.

*You can release tension in any part of your body.*
*You control the switch. Release and breathe.*

Once again, tense the sphincter muscle in the genitals.
Hold it. As you do, squeeze your buttocks together.
Feel the tension.
Release . . . and breathe.

You can tense or release any part of your body.
You can release tension in your body . . . or your mind.
It's your choice.

*Think cat's feet.*
*Release and breathe.*


Relaxing the body: toes and feet

Lastly, curl your toes and make fists with your feet.
Feel the tension in the toes and feet.
Hold it (three to four seconds).
(Curling and tensing your feet like this is like a bird,
holding onto a perch.)
Now, release... and breathe.
Think soft feet... "cat's feet."
Feel a sense of spring and balance in the pads on the soles
of your feet, and your toes.


Once again create "bird's feet."
Hold it (three to four seconds).
Release and breathe.
Experience having a comfortable, relaxed, supportive base.
Think "cat's feet."

The purpose of tensing and releasing your muscles
is not just to release tension in a few isolated muscle groups,
but to enhance your overall awareness and control.
After you've practiced tension-release five or ten times,
you no longer have to tense your muscles in order to
release them. Simply scan the body, release and breathe.

Scanning is an abbreviation of the tension-release process.
It involves tuning in to specific parts of the body, recreating
the feeling of letting go, and then releasing tension in that
area. It's just tune in... release and breathe.

*Scan, release and breathe.*

To begin, take a breath or two.
Guide attention to your hands.
Remember the feeling of release in the hands...
and take a breath.

Guide attention to your neck and shoulders.
Recall the feeling of letting go that you experienced after
raising them up.
Release and breathe.

Guide your attention to your jaw.
Release and breathe.

Allow your chest and abdomen to be free to expand (rise)
and contract (fall) with each wave of your breath.

Guide attention to your genitals.
Release any unnecessary tension in your sexual organs...
and breathe.

Guide attention to your feet.
Think "cat's feet."
Release... and breathe.

With practice, the whole scanning-release process can take
just two or three **seconds**.

## USING RELEASE

A common response to tension is to "fight it."
In so doing, people usually create more tension.
If you experience part of your body as "tense,"
don't fight or try to avoid it.
Instead, acknowledge it:
guide your attention to it.
Use it as a stimulus to trigger your "release reflex."
Release. . . and breathe.

With each breath, think of drawing in energy. . .
and sending it out through the body.
Be especially aware of allowing it to flow to and through
those areas where you habitually store and hold tension.
Use tension as a stimulus for more ease and flow.
With practice, you can release tension in any part of
your body.
You can release tension in your body or your mind.

## TURN THE WHEEL

Imagine this situation:
It's something important.
You really want to do well.
You're trying hard, perhaps too hard.
You know that "squeezing" harder doesn't really help
but you want to do a good job.
And wanting sometimes gets translated into trying
and pushing too much.
What's different now is that when you experience yourself
tensing and over-efforting you remind yourself
that **ease is power.**
You focus on breathing in energy, drawing in power. . .
and you send a wave of energy out through the body.

Experience the process once again.
Do a quick scan: release in the hands, shoulders,
abdomen, genitals, and feet.
Tune into your breathing. . . draw in energy.
Remind yourself that ease is power and that you control the
switch. Then, bring that awareness into the moment.
As you do, you'll bring a more relaxed and charged you
into any situation.

## POWER BREAK

It's been a very busy, stressful day.
You've really been pushing it,
and there's still a lot more to do.
You are starting to get irritable.
You have time for a short break,
and you're going to use the time to relax.

Sit back.
Tune into your breathing.
As you do, you begin to calm down and ease up.
Release tension in your favorite tension holding areas:
the neck and shoulders, the abdomen, and the genitals.
Remind yourself that you deserve to feel good...
and that you control the switch.
Release... and breathe.
As you breathe, remember you have a personal connection
to an unlimited supply of energy.
Draw in some of that energy...
send it out through the body.
Especially send it out to those areas that feel tense
and tired.

After five minutes, stop.
The "power break" is over.
Allow yourself to feel more relaxed and at ease.
Shift your focus back to your work.

Ease is power.
Experience yourself with more energy.
Experience yourself feeling more calm and clear.
Experience yourself able to work more efficiently.

# RELAX THE MIND

As I see it, the mind is like a t.v. set:
        it watches one channel at a time
        and you control the switch.

        If you don't like what you're watching,
        if it doesn't give you power or pleasure,
        change channels.
        You control the switch.

The key to "changing channels," to calming and clearing
the mind is to release and breathe. It's the same release
and breathe process that we used to relax the body.
Releasing and breathing reduces the emotion associated
with negative or limiting thoughts... and enables you to
let them go.
It clears the screen on your mental t.v.
Then it's important to focus on a positive, relaxing, and
empowering thought, image, or feeling.

Something I said earlier bears repeating.
Mind and body are one.
Each doubting, negative, and limiting thought creates a
reciprocal tensing or holding (however slight) in the body.

The key to "changing channels,"
to calming and clearing the mind,
is to release... breathe... refocus....

# CREATE RELAXING THOUGHTS, IMAGES, AND FEELINGS

*Think relaxed.*
*You get more*
*of what you think about.*

## RELAXING THOUGHTS

A guiding principle is you get more of what you
think about.
If you focus on tension and limitation, you create more
that is tense and limiting.
Instead, think relaxing and empowering thoughts,
In so doing, you create more ease and more power.
A key to making dynamic relaxation work for you is to
release... breathe... and bring to mind a thought like:

"I'm the boss."

"I control the switch."

"The waves never rush."

"There's time enough for me."

"I deserve my time."

"I deserve to feel good."

"I deserve to express all my ability."

"I inspire myself."

"I am response-able."

*Think relaxing and empowering thoughts.*

Select or create five or six thoughts that will really relax
and empower you.
Write them down.
Then, whenever you feel tense, anxious, negative, or
stressed. . . "change channels".
Take a breath, release, and think one of your "power
thoughts."

## RELAXING IMAGES

It's been said that imagination is the most powerful quality
of the mind and that a picture is worth a thousand words.

Put your imagination to work for you.
As you relax and breathe, imagine yourself feeling
comfortable.
Experience yourself breathing easily.
Give yourself time.
Draw in power.
Experience your body as relaxed (loose).
Imagine all systems functioning smoothly, easily, and
effectively, including those areas where you
characteristically experience more stress.
Relax and breathe.

Whether at work or play,
imagine your whole being at ease and powerful.
Imagine yourself relaxed, aware, and in the moment.
You deserve to feel good.
You deserve to express your abilities.

*A picture's worth a thousand words.*
*Imagine yourself calm and at ease.*

Some relaxation programs encourage people to take a half hour "break" to imagine themselves in a special, favorite place, a retreat where they can feel completely relaxed, at peace, and free from the stresses and pressures of life.

For some people that means imagining themselves
by a mirror-calm mountain lake
where they used to go as a child....
Or sitting alone watching the waves on a quiet beach....
For others it's lying in bed under the covers
feeling secure and at peace.

Escaping to any of these imagined retreats can provide
a pleasant and stress-reducing respite to life...
and as such it's beneficial.

Our approach to relaxation focuses more on this moment and on providing you with a way to experience more ease **while** doing whatever it is you want to do.

*When you feel tension, pressure, or stress...*
*release and breathe.*

When you are able to imagine yourself relaxed and at ease
in comfortable surroundings... then, imagine yourself
feeling relaxed and breathing easily in a more demanding,
high-pressure situation.

Think of a situation that has been stressful or anxiety
producing for you in the past, or one that you anticipate
to be stressful in the future.
Then, imagine yourself taking time to breathe, drawing in
energy and feeling comfortable and competent.
Imagine yourself "under pressure" ... and at ease.
As you do, remember, you deserve to feel good.

You'll feel better and perform better
by taking a moment to release, breathe, and refocus.
You control the switch.

If you are worrying about something you may have to do in the future, relax and breathe, **then** imagine yourself excelling in that situation.

Relaxing and breathing improves both the clarity and quality of your thoughts and images. Having clear, powerful images ("programs") will increase confidence, and strengthen your ability to express yourself in any situation. So, relax, breathe, and image.

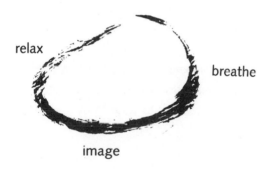

relax

breathe

image

In the arts, business, and sport, people use imagery and mental rehearsal to improve their performance. To do that, define exactly what you want to do. . . . Imagine what would be ideal. . . . Script it out. Then relax, breathe, and image yourself excelling.

*Dis-ease is generated by anxiety,*
*by feelings of separation,*
*and by a sense of being without.*

## RELAXING FEELINGS

Relax and breathe.
A key to dynamic relaxation is experiencing relaxed feelings.
Relaxed feelings are what this book is about.

Relaxed feelings include a **feeling of time**.
The waves never rush.
Give yourself time for the inbreath to come all the way in.
Give yourself time for the outbreath to go all the way out.
You deserve your time.

Relaxed feelings include a **feeling of control**.
You can release tension in any part of your body.
You can release tension in your body . . . or your mind.

Don't fight tension.
**Use it** as a reminder to release . . . and breathe.
Change channels.
Tune into the release and breathe channel.
You control the switch.

Relaxed feelings can include a **feeling of warmth**.
Some techniques focus on feeling warmth in the hands
and feet. . . and saying to yourself, "warm hands. . .
warm feet".
Warmth means energy (and blood flow).
Some people have learned to turn off migraine and tension
headaches just by relaxing, breathing, and creating feelings
of warmth in their hands and feet.

Relax, breathe, and stream warm energy out
through the body.
Stream it down through the pelvis and the legs, into the
soles of your feet and toes. Think warm feet. . . cat's feet.

Relax, breathe, and allow a warm, soothing energy to
stream through your shoulders and arms, into the palms of
your hands and fingers. Think warm hands.

Relax, breathe and stream a warm, soothing energy up the
spinal column into your head and eyes.
(The spinal column is the power cable in the body.)
Experience a subtle, lengthening effect in the spinal column.

The hands, feet, and eyes are all well represented in the
sensory cortex of the brain. Streaming a warm, soothing
energy out to these five areas is relaxing and integrating.

You can enrich your experience by coloring the energy you stream out through the body.

If you are feeling angry or irritable,
relax, breathe, and stream a cool, clear, light **blue** energy through your body.

If you feel frustrated and confused,
allow a cool, soothing **green** energy
to flow through your body.

If you are feeling alone or afraid,
relax, breathe, and stream a soft, warm, **rose** or **gold**en energy through your body.

Experience the differences of temperature and color.
Allow yourself to feel good.
Allow energy to stream through you.

Communion means to experience a sense of union
and connectedness.
To experience a greater sense of communion
relax... breathe... and allow energy to stream to you
and through you.
You deserve to feel good.

## REFOCUSING USING RELAXING THOUGHTS,
## IMAGES, AND FEELINGS

Imagine that you are rushing.
You're in a real hurry.
However, circumstances are that you have to wait.
Suddenly a stranger cuts in front of you in a line
or in traffic.
You feel yourself tighten up and experience a rush of anger.

Imagine yourself standing or sitting there upset,
with anger and tension building....
You know that feeling.
It's the same feeling you've had
when you've been criticized inappropriately
or treated disrespectfully in the past.
You feel like you're about to react impulsively
and aggressively... to explode.

Then, you perceive what's happening to you.
You realize you're making yourself upset...
and that's neither productive nor pleasurable.
You think "change channels."
You tune into your breathing.
You release some of the tension.
You "clear the screen."

"Clearing the screen" allows you to refocus.
It enables you to think a calming, clearing, empowering thought; something like, "I don't need someone (who's insensitive, ignorant, or uptight) to treat me respectfully for me to feel good about myself.
I control the switch."

Then, if you're in line and you want to do something about the situation, you calmly and clearly inform the stranger to get to the back of the line.

Research sometimes suggests things we can do
to improve the quality of our lives...
though it's still up to us to do it.

Research findings indicate that people who upset
themselves easily are three to four times more prone
to having a heart attack than those who don't.

Research findings also indicate that people who have had
heart attacks, who learn how to relax
and avoid upsetting themselves
are forty per cent less likely to have another attack
than those who don't.

Learning to release... breathe... and refocus
will allow you to respond with more ease and intelligence,
instead of reacting thoughtlessly and reflexively,
it will enable you to tap the wisdom
that comes from a broadened perspective.
It will enable you to reduce stress,
and feel good.

You deserve to feel good.
You deserve to express all your ability.

# A LITTLE RELAXATION...

# THREE WAYS TO RELAX

The three elements of dynamic relaxation are:

RELAXED BREATHING...
breathing with rhythm, ease, and power.

RELAXED BODY...
enhancing your ability to release tension.

RELAXED MIND...
refocusing on relaxing thoughts, images, and feelings.

Three ways to effectively put these elements to use are:

INSTANT RELEASE...
a two to three second release, breath, refocus reflex.

AN EASY MOMENT...
a two to three minute release-recharge process.

A POWER BREAK...
a five minute relaxation break.

*Release... breathe... refocus.*
*Use tension to trigger your release reflex.*

**INSTANT RELEASE** is the essence of dynamic relaxation.
Whenever you perceive yourself as tense, or find yourself
thinking a negative, anxious, or limiting thought,
**use** the tension and negativity as a stimulus
to release... breathe... and refocus.
Focus on a relaxing thought,
a relaxing image,
or a relaxing feeling.
You control the switch.

Instant release is a powerful form of meditation.
One that will change negative thoughts into positive ones,
or your tense thoughts into relaxed ones. To do it,
all you have to do is release... breathe... and refocus.

Instant release demands awareness and discipline.
It demands that each time you become aware you're
tensing or thinking a tense, limiting thought,
you use it to release... breathe... and refocus.
Eventually, the negatives become positives...
and you become freer and more effective.

Avoid getting emotionally caught up in
tension and negativity.
Remember, feeling good is natural.
You deserve to feel good.
And, you control the switch.

Taking a couple of seconds to release, breathe, and refocus
throughout the day minimizes the build up of tension
and keeps you lighter and more at ease.

*Distinguish what you can control*
*from what you can't.*
*Release what you can't control.*
*Refocus on the positive.*

We all enjoy the feeling of being appreciated, well thought
of, and respected. That's natural.

Imagine something undesirable is happening. . .
or has happened.
Though it's not your fault, you're concerned and worried
about what **others** may be thinking.
It's causing you some tension and embarrassment.
You feel uncomfortable.
And you're letting it interfere with your well-being
as well as your behavior.

As you become aware of what's happening you know what to do. . . .
Be natural.
Use the situation you're in as an opportunity to be freer and more positive.
Focus on releasing and breathing.
Change channels.
Say to yourself, "I'm o.k. I don't need _____ to happen to feel good about myself." or, "I don't need _____'s approval to feel relaxed or o.k."
I control the switch.

Then, tune into feeling good.

*Are you concerned that others might be saying*
*unpleasant things about you?*
*Of course they are. Some people will say unpleasant*
*things about everyone. So what?*

A key to relaxing the mind is distinguishing what you can control from what you can't. When it comes to dealing with things outside your control (like what someone else might be thinking about you) don't worry and upset yourself about it. Don't let it use you. Instead, use it.

Use doubt as a reminder to release, breathe, and refocus.
Focus on being at ease, calm, and power full.
Remember, you deserve to feel good.
And, you control the switch.

Throughout the day, and whenever you experience tension, anxiety, limitation, and dis-ease, practice a little instant release.

Release, breathe, and refocus.
You control the switch.

*Connect the inbreath to the outbreath...*
*The outbreath to the inbreath... twenty times.*


**AN EASY MOMENT** is more than just a reflex-like response to tension, where you take a second or two to release... breathe... refocus. Nor is it a time out or an escape.

An easy moment is a two to three **minute** break in the action where you can release and recharge.

It involves scanning the body (shoulders, neck, jaw, abdomen, genitals, and feet) and releasing;

especially in your favorite tension-holding spots.

Then, it's tuning into your breathing, taking your time, drawing in power, and counting

**twenty "connected" breaths.**

A "connected breath" involves breathing in energy . . .
all the way in until the inbreath becomes an outbreath.
Then it's allowing the outbreath to flow all the way out . . .
until the outbreath becomes an inbreath.

Repeat the cycle; breathing in until the inbreath becomes
an outbreath . . . and out until the outbreath becomes an
inbreath. And so on . . . for twenty "connected" breaths.

As you breathe, take your time, and think thoughts like,
"I deserve my time."
"The waves never rush."

Breathe easy.
Draw in energy.
Stream it out.
And think thoughts like,
"I have a personal connection to an unlimited supply
of energy."
"Energy flows to me and through me."
"I have everything I need to enjoy this moment."
"I deserve to express my ability."

Most of the people I work with rush, push, and squeeze too much. By remembering to bring more ease to the moment, you will feel better and play at a higher level . . . longer.

As you breathe, think thoughts like,
"Release and breathe."
"I deserve to feel good."
"I have everything I need to enjoy my here and now."
"I control the switch."

After twenty counts of breathing and thinking two or three relaxing thoughts, change channels and return to the moment of what's happening out there.
AN EASY MOMENT is a mini release-recharge break.
It's a brief, high-quality form of
re-creation that I recommend my clients experience several times a day.

## POWER BREAK

Throughout the book I've described a number of techniques for breathing, releasing, and refocusing. These three elements can also be used in a single five to ten minute "power break". It's a very effective relaxation technique. One that I've used in working with some of the world's most high-pressured performers. And it's something **you** can use to feel more comfortable and to perform with greater effectiveness and ease.

RELAX AND BREATHE
Sit or lie back and make yourself comfortable.
Uncross your arms and your legs.
Allow the weight of your body to be supported.
Allow your spinal column to be straight.

BREATHE EASY
Give yourself time for the inbreath to become an outbreath.
Draw in energy. . . . and release.
Experience the continuous wave after wave
quality of the breath.

SCAN AND RELEASE
Allow the hands, shoulders, neck, abdomen, genitals, and
feet to relax.
As you release . . . breathe in energy.


Then on the outbreath send it out to those parts of your
body that feel especially tense or tired.
(For example, if you feel tension in your neck, bring your
awareness to that area. Release and breathe in energy.
Then, on the outbreath allow a warm soothing energy to
flow up into your neck, subtly lengthen the spinal column,
and allow the muscles to relax.)

## A RELAXED FOCUS

There are many ways to relax the body and calm the mind.
One that I've found to be both effective and pleasurable is
to tune into the breathing; especially the point where the
breath changes direction.
As other thoughts and feelings come to mind, observe
them . . . and let them go. Then guide your attention back
to the breath.
Experience the breath as turning a wheel.
Let your breath be your focus.
Let your focus be your breath.

Relax and breathe.
Experience your time.
Experience energy flowing to you and through you.
Experience the point where the breath changes direction.
Experience ease as you breathe.
Experience this breath.

For the next ten minutes relax and breathe.
Relax and recharge.

*Relax and breathe.*

A Little Relaxation. . . . .

Re-lax means to regain a natural feeling of looseness.
Relaxing is an experience. It's something to **do**.
It's not just something to understand.

You can relax whenever you feel tense, stressed, tired. . .
and whenever you want to.

You can do it in an instant simply by releasing,
taking a breath (or two), and refocusing.

You can do it in a moment or two by experiencing twenty
"connected" breaths, scanning, releasing tension, and
thinking a few relaxing thoughts.

Or. . .
you can relax with a "power break" — a five or ten minute
time out from the stress and pressure of the day.

What's important is that you do it.
That you release, breathe, and focus on ease and power.
You can use any style, but remember to use tension
as a stimulus to release. . . breathe. . . and turn the wheel.

You deserve to feel good.
You deserve to express all your ability.
You control the switch.

# A DYNAMIC RELAXATION LIFESTYLE

Imagine yourself seated in a darkened room.
It is calm and quiet.
A candle burns emitting a steady, golden glow.
You feel peaceful.

Then, a breeze cuts through the room.
As it does the candle flickers.
Your focus shifts.
The feeling in the room changes.

An ideal is to live your life
so that you are calm and quiet within,
and less affected by each passing breeze
and the flickering of a candle.


Many things impact on us. The impact can be
overwhelming. The way we live our lives can have a
profound effect on our capacity to react with more ease
and less stress.
Four factors that can enhance your ability to relax are:
diet, recreation, attitude, and relationship.

*Of all the factors that affect us
there's none that's more basic
and over which we have greater control
than what we put into our mouths,
and the mouths of our children.*

## DIET

North Americans eat far too much. They especially eat too much fat, too much protein, too much meat, too much sugar, and too many processed and highly refined foods. There's no doubt about it, what we eat affects how we feel, think, and act. If you eat like a lion, or consume lots of sugar or coffee, you stress your system and make it much more difficult to feel calm and relaxed.

I spent several years researching and writing a book *Food For Thought: A New Look at Food and Behavior,* (Prentice-Hall) on the relationship of food and behavior. I've discovered that the quality of the energy we put into our mouths as food directly affects the quality of energy we express as behavior.

A whole range of behavior problems, including emotional upsets and outbursts, addiction, hyperactivity, hypertension, some forms of sexual dysfunction, educational problems, and even criminal behavior can be significantly reduced by experiencing a change in diet, learning to relax, and "controlling the switch".

I go along with the intelligent and prevalent advice of the times, which recommends a high-fiber, low fat, moderate protein, and low sugar diet. But don't just take the expert's advice. Become more sensitive to how the food you eat affects **you**. And eat less of those foods that leave you feeling heavy, tired, nervous, depressed, or irritable.

In *Food For Thought,* I told the story of an elderly man I met in my travels in Greece. The old fellow had tremendous energy. As I was studying the relationship of food and behavior, I asked him if there were any special dietary recommendations he might share that promote well-being and longevity.
"No," he replied, "None." Though his diet was simple, he went on to add that he ate a little of almost everything.
"And there's no advice that you'd be willing to pass on?" I asked.
There was a long pause, then he said, "Well, there is one thing. . . if I eat something and it makes me sick, I rarely eat it again."

Become more sensitive to how the food you eat
affects you.
Eat those foods that allow you to feel more calm
and centered.
Avoid those foods that contribute to your experiencing
tension and dis-ease.

---

An environmental note: None of us lives in a vacuum. It's
important to be aware that what's stressful for you can also
have a significant impact on the world around you. Regarding
diet, the excessive consumption of meat, sugar, and coffee
stresses the ecosystem as well as the individual. . . . And
stressing the environment ultimately sets up a condition that
stresses us all.

*Enjoy relaxing forms of recreation.*

## RECREATION

Re-creation means to regenerate; to make anew. It's beneficial to both your well-being and your productivity to develop healthy forms of recreation.

Exercise is marvellous recreation. It's a balance to sitting and thinking. A way to tone the body, and a wonderful antedote to insomnia and many forms of dis-ease. Two keys to recreational exercise are that it's enjoyable, and that it's somewhat regular. (Most experts seem to suggest three to four twenty minute exercise sessions per week, as a minimum.)

Almost all kinds of exercise are fine. Walking, jogging (if you don't beat yourself up), golf, tennis, cycling, yoga, dance, aerobics (again, if you don't beat yourself up), racquet sports, and team games are all fine and fun.

Your exercise can be vigorous or moderate. If it's vigorous you should build up to it. And remember, don't get too serious about it. If you set performance standards and goals that are too aggressive, and if your recreation gets too competitive, it becomes tensing and stressful... instead of renewing.

There are many other forms of recreation which can be very relaxing. Some of my favorites include walking, t'ai chi, music (both listening and playing), painting and drawing, sitting by a fire, humor, conversation and making love.

Watching t.v. is the most popular form of recreation in North America. For most people t.v. is more of a diversion or an escape than a true form of recreation. And, don't kid yourself, watching sport on t.v. isn't nearly as re-creational as playing or participating in something yourself.

*And thou shalt love thy neighbour as thyself.*

## ATTITUDE

An attitude is a predisposition to respond.
It's a way you think and feel that affects how you relate
and react to the world around you. If you think everyone's
out to get you, then you predispose yourself to react
defensively... and contract.
If you are more self-loving and at ease, you tend to look at
difficulties and challenges as opportunities... and move
forward.

Attitudes (like most things) can be changed. One thing you
can do that will give you a greater sense of ease and
confidence, is to remind yourself **frequently** to breathe easy
and think self-appreciative thoughts like, "I deserve my
time," "I deserve to feel good," "I deserve to express my
abilities," "I don't need everyone to approve of me all the
time for me to feel good about myself," and "I control the
switch."

With time and practice, your awareness will grow. Your attitude will become more calm, more self-loving, and more confident. As it does, you'll predispose yourself to feeling even more comfortable and at ease.

After all, why shouldn't you feel at ease?
It's natural.
It feels good.
It enhances your well-being.
It enables you to relate with more effectiveness and joy.
And, you control the switch.

*Relax with others.*

## RELATIONSHIP

Last but not least is relationship.
By that I mean how we get along with others at home, at work, and at play.

Probably the most tensing and stressful aspect of relationships is trying to control others' behavior. We all do it. Parents try to control their children, husbands try to control their wives, management tries to control labor, and friends and associates try to control each other. Indeed, the closer we are, the more it seems we invest ourselves in controlling the behavior of that significant other... and the more we upset ourselves when they don't appear to listen.

For our purposes, the "why we do it" isn't so important. What is important is that we have an expectation of how we want them to be to us, and when they're not that way we upset ourselves about it.

I remember a man saying to me with emotion, "My wife really makes me sick."
"Where do you feel it?" I asked.
"When I'm at home with her," he commented "all the time."
"No" I asked "where in your body do you feel it?"
He thought for a moment, then he replied "In my gut (abdomen) and my chest."
"Your wife's not in there," I explained. "She doesn't upset you. It's you who upset yourself."

It's not unreasonable to have preferences, and to want the people you live and work with to treat and react to you in a certain way. However, when you start upsetting yourself because they're not responding to you exactly the way you want them to, that's not a preference, that's an addiction.

The solution to this, and to many addictions is what I've been saying all along. It's what will support you in feeling good and expressing a more positive attitude in the moment. It's to release... breathe... and refocus. Think, "I don't need him, her, or them to treat me (to behave) the way I think they should for me to feel good about myself. I'm o.k." And "I control the switch."

Changing addictions to preferences in relationships makes life easier... and a lot more pleasurable.

*A Little Relaxation*... is about releasing, breathing,
thinking, and living.
It's about being with ease.


Practicing a little relaxation is easy.
It requires your interest, your awareness, and your ability to
"change channels."
It's remembering to release... breathe... refocus,
that you deserve to feel good...
and that you control the switch.


Remember, repetition builds strength. The program is
designed so that you can read this book again and again.
As you read, release and breathe.

# THE AUTHOR

DR. SAUL MILLER is a psychologist who consults in sport, business, the professions, and the arts. His clients have included: the New York Mets, the Los Angeles Rams, Dodgers, and Kings, 1984 and '88 Olympic teams, and PGA tour golfers. His principal role with all these performers is to provide input and techniques that assist them in being more effective and more at ease.

Dr. Miller conducts performance seminars throughout the United States and Canada, bringing his techniques to people in all walks of life. He is the author of *Performing Under Pressure* (1991), and *Food For Thought: A New Look at Food and Behavior* (Prentice-Hall, 1979).

Dr. Miller has a doctorate (Ph.D. clinical psychology) from the Institute of Psychiatry, University of London (England), and has trained in the Alexander Technique and Eastern disciplines. His skill as a facilitator is widely appreciated. In the past, the Mets called him "Dr.Bombay" (after the doctor in t.v.'s "Bewitched" who was called in when the witches lost their powers), the Rams called him "Yoda" (after the Jedi master of Star Wars fame who wisely counselled Luke Skywalker), some of his clients have called him "the guru," "the head coach," and "the Wizard of Ease."

In *A Little Relaxation* he describes a dynamic relaxation technique that he developed and has effectively put to use with some of the world's top performers. It is something that has value for us all.